the generosity ladder

YOUR NEXT STEP TO FINANCIAL PEACE

nelson searcy

WITH JENNIFER DYKES HENSON

BakerBooks

a division of Baker Publishing Group
Grand Rapids, Michigan

© 2010 by Nelson Searcy

Published by Baker Books
a division of Baker Publishing Group
P.O. Box 6287, Grand Rapids, MI 49516-6287
www.bakerbooks.com

Printed in the United States of America

Library of Congress Cataloging-in-Publication Data
Searcy, Nelson.
    The generosity ladder : your next step to financial peace / Nelson
    Searcy with Jennifer Dykes Henson.
        p.   cm.
    Includes bibliographical references.
    ISBN 978-0-8010-7276-5 (pbk.)
    1. Generosity—Religious aspects—Christianity. 2. Christian giv-
    ing. I. Henson, Jennifer Dykes. II. Title.
    BV4647.G45S43 2010
    241′.4—dc22   2010016790

10   11   12   13   14   15   16   7   6   5   4   3   2   1

contents

acknowledgments

I would like to dedicate this book to Alexander Searcy, my son. May God entrust you with the true riches of heaven.

My thanks to Jesus Christ for giving me the grace to climb the generosity ladder, even though I stumble badly at times. I also would like to thank each of these individuals for their contributions to this book: Kelley Searcy, Jennifer Dykes Henson, Kerrick Thomas, Jason Haltey, Scott Whitaker, Tommy Duke, Cristina Fowler, Chad Allen, Vinny Bove, and all the pastors, writers, and teachers who have influenced my understanding of biblical stewardship.

Nelson Searcy

Thanks to God for giving us all such a clear plan for financial stewardship. May we learn to approach money as he intends and in doing so find the freedom to pursue his true desires. Thanks, Nelson, for inviting me into this critical work.

Jennifer Dykes Henson

welcome to your new reality

Dream with me for a moment. Relax and imagine a reality in which:

- You don't live with financial strain.
- You don't struggle to make ends meet each month.
- You are completely out of debt.
- You aren't bound by the ties of materialism.
- Your needs are consistently met.
- You have the ability to save for your children's education and your retirement.
- You have the desire and ability to help people in need.

- You have the resources to give to causes much bigger than your own concerns.
- You live a life full of generosity, joy, and peace.

The principles contained in this little book have the potential to turn these dreams into a reality. Whether or not they will depends on what you decide to do with them. Your next step to financial peace begins with discovering how to scale the generosity ladder. As we get started, I make you this promise: the view from the top rung is well worth the climb.

Are you ready?

1

shifting perspectives

The way we see things is the source of the way we think and the way we act.

Stephen Covey

Have you ever experienced a paradigm shift? You know, that moment of clarity when you realize there's an entirely different way of seeing things than the way you've always seen them?

The first step in experiencing a paradigm shift is to acknowledge that you currently see the world through a certain set of lenses. These lenses have been created by a number of factors—your family, your upbringing, your education, and your social circle, to name a few. Based on your life experience, you understand the world in a specific way. Or as Shakespeare penned, "Such as we are made of, such we be." I would take the liberty of adding "and such we see" to the great writer's assertion.

The concept of a paradigm shift first came on the scene in 1962 with Thomas Kuhn's work *The Structure of Scientific Revolutions.* Kuhn exposed the reality that nearly every noteworthy advancement in science is, at its core, a break with an old way of seeing the world. His revelation proved that to make strides toward any kind of advancement, we must first recognize our current paradigms and then open ourselves up to the possibility of a new way of thinking.

Perhaps the best way to illustrate this phenomenon is with an actual illustration. Go ahead and take a look at figure 1.1 on the next page.

Depending on your perspective, you may see a beautiful young woman shyly turning her face away from the artist, or you may see an old, hunched woman with a large nose and downcast gaze. Which woman do you see? Whichever one it is, another reality exists.

If you see the young woman in the picture, I have news for you: this is a picture of an old lady. But to see her, you have to shift your perspective. Here are some clues to help you see things a new way: the young woman's ear is the older woman's eye. The curve of her chin is the tip of the old woman's nose. Do you see her yet? One more hint: the choker necklace around the younger subject's neck is the opening of the old woman's mouth. (If you first saw the older woman, just work backward from these clues until you see the younger woman's image.)

Pretty amazing, huh? I have seen people get angry with one another over this exercise. Sometimes those

Fig. 1.1. What Do You See?

who see the old woman first are so convinced they are right that they think those seeing something else are crazy. And vice versa. We all tend to think we see things as they really are, but obviously that's not the case. This image is a trivial example, but it illustrates a profound truth: when we are able to open our minds to a new reality, we give ourselves the opportunity to experience life-changing, growth-spurring paradigm shifts.

Money Matters

Most of us have grown up with a skewed understanding of money and possessions. Based on misinformation, poor examples, and our own desires, we have unconsciously developed a certain paradigm for understanding and managing our income—from the first $5 bill we were given in a birthday card to our first paycheck, and everything we've received since. Unfortunately, for most of us, our financial paradigm has led us into trouble. Our collective wrong perspective has landed us as a society in major debt and contributed to broken families and high levels of stress and anxiety.

Our intentions to handle our resources well may be good, but money in our culture has gone bad. Too many people feel they have to go into debt just to meet their basic needs. Every day is a struggle. Others simply want to go on a nice vacation or give their kids a good education. We want to take care of our aging parents or save for our retirement. But we can't get around to doing these things because we lack the funds.

The majority of us—incredibly wealthy by the world's standards—are locked in a battle with the constant desire for more. Don't think you are wealthy? If you make more than $2 a day, you are among the top 2 percent of the wealthiest people in the world. Yet even in our abundance, we have internalized the "buy now, pay later" mantra of our culture. We live above our means.

As my friend and financial guru Dave Ramsey says, "We buy things we don't need with money we don't have to impress people we don't even like." Have you ever been there? Money has become a way of keeping score. It's as if we are in competition with each other to see who can get the most stuff, live in the biggest house, and wear the most expensive clothes.

While different people experience different levels of financial need, money is a continual struggle for us all.

No matter how much we have, we always seem to need more. Financial stress is a shadow that never seems to leave us.

Most of our money problems boil down to bad financial decisions—financial decisions that are the result of a distorted perspective. In fact, we are often so rooted in our own paradigm of money management that we don't even realize we are making poor decisions. Like a fish in water, we can't see the reality of the environment around

---

Most of our money problems boil down to bad financial decisions—financial decisions that are the result of a distorted perspective.

---

us. We are just doing what we know to do, wondering why we continually live under the thumb of financial oppression.

To get back on the right track, we need a good dose of self-examination. Take a look at your own financial life. Here are a few signs that you are not making wise financial decisions:

- Your debt is growing each month.

- You are making only the minimum monthly payments to your creditors.

- If you miss one paycheck, you can't cover your mortgage/rent and bills.

- You and your spouse fight about money regularly. (By the way, money problems are the number-one cause of divorce in America.)

- You are not able to put money into a savings or retirement account every month.

- You are constantly stressed about money.

- Because of your financial situation, you feel like you can't live the life you were created to live.

Can you relate to any of these warning signs? If you are like most people I talk with—most people I've met— you can relate to practically all of them.

By and large, we live in a place of financial uncertainty. We aren't able to do all the things we should do, much less the things we want to do, because we are bound by money-colored handcuffs. But why? How did we create a world in which financial stress and unrelenting scarcity are the new norm? By operating out of our own financial paradigms. I'd say it's time for a shift in perspective.

What Is the Generosity Ladder?

If you've ever changed a light bulb or painted a house, you know that a ladder is simply a tool to get you from your current level to a higher plane. Things that are out of reach before we step onto a ladder are easily in our grasp after we climb to the top.

The generosity ladder, like any ladder, is a tool. Right now you are standing at the bottom of the ladder, ankle deep in the financial stress of debt, anxiety, and frustration, looking toward the top rung, the place from which you'll be able to wrap your hand around a life filled with financial peace (see fig. 1.2).

From that top rung, the new reality you've been dreaming of will be fully within your reach. But before you can start the climb toward a better future, you have to do two things:

1. Acknowledge that your current way of viewing and managing your money isn't getting you where you want to be financially.
2. Commit to questioning your own paradigm and beginning to see your financial life through a different lens.

Fig. 1.2. The Generosity Ladder:
Your Tool for Financial Peace

The journey toward financial peace begins with a paradigm shift. Just as you had to change your perspective to see the old woman (or the young woman) in figure 1, you need to change your perspective in regard to the dollar bills in your bank account.

Perhaps right now you feel like money has control over you. That's because your paradigm is giving it con-

---

Doing more of what you've always done will only get you more of what you've always gotten.

---

trol. Perhaps you are convinced that you'll never have enough. That's because your paradigm has led you to this false belief. Maybe you are so far in debt that you can't see a way out. Your paradigm got you there.

When you shift your perspective, you will experience a financial transformation. But the key is to allow yourself to see your money in a different light. As you read this book, let me encourage you to stay open to the ideas I am presenting. You will have to step into some uncomfortable territory. Change is never easy. When you've been operating by one set of beliefs for a long time, it can be difficult to open yourself up to a new set. But just remember—doing more of what you've always done will only get you more of what you've always gotten.

Here's what I can guarantee: if you take this climb up the generosity ladder, you will experience life as you've never known it before. You will finally be able to replace financial stress with financial peace. You will be free to live the life you've been created to live, without the weight of constant worry. But you have to be willing to let the lens of truth clarify your perspective, starting with one big, underlying, paradigm-shifting truth: God owns it all.

Everything was created through him and for him.

Colossians 1:16

2

stepping toward excellence

Our stewardship of our money and possessions becomes the story of our lives.

Randy Alcorn

Have you ever sat up all night on Christmas Eve, or the night before a big birthday, and put together one of those "assembly required" toys for a child? Do you remember the feeling of excitement? Finally you would give her the one thing she wanted more than anything else. Maybe you had to go all over town to find the gift and pay more than you really wanted to, but you didn't mind because you couldn't wait to give your child the desire of her heart.

Not too long ago I had this experience with my young son. He had a birthday coming up, and he wanted one specific toy more than he had wanted anything else in his life. The only problem was that the toy was new and incredibly popular, which meant it was in short supply.

During my lunch break on the afternoon before his birthday, I set out on a mission to find the one gift that would make my son the happiest boy in the world. After running in and out of stores all over the city, I finally found exactly what I was looking for. But it cost nearly twice as much as I had expected. What did I do? Yep, like any good father, I bought my son the toy anyway.

I didn't even realize the thing needed assembling until I got home late that evening. So after the almost-birthday boy was tucked into bed, I worked into the wee hours screwing together chunks of plastic. When I was finished, I left the surprise in the middle of the living room floor, so it would be the first thing my son saw on his birthday.

Needless to say, the next morning he was ecstatic. I have never seen so much jumping up and down and squealing with delight. His attention was glued to this toy that represented so much of my time, effort, and money. I was happy I had been able to give him a good gift. His joy was all the gratitude I needed.

Well, as happens more often than I'd like to admit, watching him play brought out the little boy in me. I decided I wanted to try out the new toy for myself.

I asked my son, "Hey, can I see that for just a minute?" Any idea what his response was?

In typical little-boy fashion he replied, "No, Daddy. It's mine."

Now, I have to admit my first thought was, "I bought you that toy, and I sat up half the night putting it together. Not to mention, I'm a lot bigger than you are. I could reach down and take it away right now. Or I could go buy you ten more, if I decided to. And you are going to tell me that it's yours?"

Of course I didn't say any of those things, but as I sat there watching my son, I couldn't help but think about how often I had treated God the same way my child had just treated me. How often have I taken the resources and gifts God has given me and set about using them for my own purposes and enjoyment with little regard for his ultimate ownership? How often have you?

Recognizing the Source

Giving is not something that comes naturally for us. We like to have complete control over our resources. After all, they are ours. We are the ones who got up and went to work for them. They sit in our bank account. We have a right to hold on to them as tightly as we'd like and to do with them as we please. Right?

Well, not exactly.

Just as I paid for and gave my son his new toy, God gives us all the financial resources that come into our lives. James 1:17 tells us, "Whatever is good and perfect comes down to us from God our Father, who created all the lights in the heavens." Everything good in our lives comes from God.

First Timothy 6:17 echoes James's words and takes things a little further: "Teach those who are rich in this world not to be proud and not to trust in their money, which is so unreliable. Their trust should be in God, who richly gives us all we need for our enjoyment." God gives us all we need. You may have worked hard for the money that has come into your life, but God gave you the breath, health, strength, and intelligence to do your job. He gave you every ounce of your ability to earn your living just as surely as I placed that toy on the living room floor for my son to find.

God richly gives us all we need *for our enjoyment*. God wants us to live blessed lives. He wants us to take pleasure in our days. Let me be clear: nothing is wrong with enjoying the fruits of our labor. We have a responsibility to provide comfortably for our family and to save for the future. God simply wants us to use our money wisely so that we have the opportunity to live well and do good for others.

First Timothy goes on to say, "Tell them to use their money to do good. They should be rich in good works and generous to those in need, always being ready to share with others. By doing this they will be storing up their treasure as a good foundation for the future so that they may experience true life" (6:18–19). The problem comes when we fail to recognize where our money and our "toys" come from, when we begin to hoard them for our own pleasure. The solution is a grace-driven paradigm shift.

If my son had realized that since I was the source of the money used to buy his birthday gift, it ultimately belonged to me, he would have been much more willing to share. But just as he did that day, we too often live under the false impression that we are the master of whatever finds its way into our hands. Eager not to let a good thing get away, we close our fist around it with no regard for the ultimate source. The only hope we have of loosening the death grip we have on our goods is to acknowledge that everything we have belongs to God.

All of our money, houses, toys, mutual funds, clothes, gadgets, stocks, and retirement plans are not really our

---

The only hope we have of loosening the death grip we have on our goods is to acknowledge that everything we have belongs to God.

---

own; they are God's. We've just been entrusted with managing the resources he pours into our lives. Whether we are overseeing huge portfolios or shoestring weekly budgets, we are all managers of God's means. That's actually where the term *stewardship* comes from.

A steward is someone who manages the wealth and property of another. The steward doesn't take ownership of his master's possessions. He doesn't use them for his own gain. He doesn't stash a little of the crop away so his family can increase their lifestyle. Instead, he distributes his master's resources as they should be distributed. Part of this means releasing a significant portion of the treasure back into the master's work.

Three Critical Questions

Understanding God's ultimate ownership means that we also recognize our role as conduits of his resources. We were not put on this earth to amass treasures for ourselves but to let treasure pass through us and back to a greater purpose. The "get all we can while we can" mind-set that most of us live with is what has driven our culture's financial health off a cliff. In our ignorance, we have turned our perspective away from God and placed it on earthly things that will pass away.

Whether we like to admit it or not, most of us live under the impression that the most important thing we can do on this earth is accumulate wealth. But by clutching our material possessions as we constantly search for more, we are fighting a battle we've already lost. When John D. Rockefeller died, he left all his wealth behind—and so will you. Not only that, but you will be held accountable for what you did with it while you were on this earth.

Paul reminds us in Romans 14:12 that one day "each of us will give a personal account to God." In 2 Corinthians 5:10, he reiterates, "For we must all stand before Christ to be judged. We will each receive whatever we deserve for the good or evil we have done in this earthly body." That goes as much for how we handled our money as anything else. Perhaps more so, especially given Jesus's affirmation in Matthew 6:21: "Wherever your treasure is, there the desires of your heart will also be."

God is examining where we are laying up our treasure while we are on this earth—or, to think of it in Jesus's

---

One day everyone must answer these three questions: Where did it all go? What did I spend it on? What has been accomplished for eternity through my use of all this wealth?"

---

terms, where the desires of our hearts are focused—and we will have to give an account. In his great work on this subject, *Money, Possessions, and Eternity*, Randy Alcorn writes, "One day everyone must answer these three questions: Where did it all go? What did I spend it on? What has been accomplished for eternity through my use of all this wealth?"[1]

And make no mistake, if you are reading this book, it's a safe bet you are wealthy by the world's standards. You may not feel like you manage a fortune, but if you are fortunate enough to have warm clothes, a roof over your head, and enough food to eat, you are extremely affluent in the grand scheme of things.

Alcorn illustrates when he says, "Take for example a man or woman who works from age twenty-five to sixty-five and makes 'only' $25,000 a year. . . . This person of modest income (by our standards) will receive a million dollars. He or she will manage a fortune."[2] How will he manage it? How will you?

Don't Be a Monkey

You may have heard the story about how people catch monkeys in India. Long ago an insightful hunter figured out that monkeys are selfish creatures, so he created a way to capture them that takes advantage of this nature.

First, the monkey hunter cuts a small hole in one end of a coconut—a hole just big enough for a monkey to fit his hand inside—and ties a long cord to the other end. Then he puts peanuts, banana chunks, or some other enticing treat into the hole. He places the coconut in the monkey's path and sneaks away, holding the other end of the cord. Inevitably, an unsuspecting monkey comes along, sniffs out the treat, and wriggles his little hand into the hole to grab the treasure. With that, the hunter's job is done. All he has to do is yank his side of the cord, and the entire monkey/coconut kit and caboodle lands at his feet.

But isn't there something missing here? Why wouldn't the monkey just pull his hand out of the coconut and run for his life? Remember that monkeys are selfish. Once they get their hands on something they want, they won't let go. With his fist wrapped around the goods, the monkey can't get his hand out of the hole. If he would just loosen his grip and let go of the bounty, he could save himself. But he clings tightfisted to what's "his" and finds himself ensnared.

It's easy for us to see how ridiculous the monkey is being. If we were sitting at the edge of the jungle watching the scenario play out, we would scream, "Let go!

That little fortune isn't worth your life!" And yet back in our own corner of the world, we are as guilty as the monkey. We hold on too tightly. We want what is ours, and we want it so badly that we are often blind to the consequences of our grasping.

We are born keen on self-preservation. Despite the seeds of generosity that may be in our heart, we all are prone to approach life with an almost primal hoarding mentality. We want to be secure. We want to get all we can. We are focused so intently on our "treasure" that we don't see the hunter lurking behind that nearby tree.

Openhanded Living

Let me place Jesus's declaration about the connection between our heart and our treasure in context:

> Don't store up treasures here on earth, where moths eat them and rust destroys them, and where thieves break in and steal. Store your treasures in heaven, where moths and rust cannot destroy, and thieves do not break in and steal. Wherever your treasure is, there the desires of your heart will also be. (Matt. 6:19–21)

If we are intent on storing up wealth for ourselves on this earth, we are acting like our primate friends. We are trading something of eternal value (treasure in heaven) for something that is ultimately of little value (treasure on earth). And as our greedy little hand stays closed over our earthly treasure, that's where our heart will be fully anchored. We all know what accompanies a life in which money takes the top priority: stress, lack, and anxiety. All the things we have too much of already.

Here's some great news: you don't have to be afraid of opening your hand and giving control of your financial life to God. There is nothing more freeing than acknowledging the truth that your money is not yours anyway and accepting your role as a steward. Changing your paradigm can change your life.

The reason so few of us have taken this step is because the topic of financial stewardship has become taboo. People in positions of leadership have long been afraid to broach the subject, which has left everyone else confused. But stewardship is a part of life. If we don't learn how to handle our resources the way God intends, we'll never be able to live the life God created us to live. So the fear has to end. Money has to be brought out of the shadows.

Jesus was never afraid to talk about money. Besides the kingdom of God, stewardship was his favorite subject. He talked more about money and possessions than

---

If we don't learn how to handle our resources the way God intends, we'll never be able to live the life God created us to live.

---

about faith and prayer combined. He spent more time dealing with denari than with heaven or hell. In fact, 2,350 verses in the Bible talk about money and how to deal with money. If I were asked to sum up all his teaching on money and possessions in one sentence, it would be this: don't be a monkey.

Just kidding. It would actually be: live an openhanded life. When you open your hand and give something that's difficult to deal with over to God, he replaces that empty space in your palm with peace. So as you learn to release control of your money to God, he will replace your financial stress with financial peace.

We can't deny the connection between our wallet and our heart. Money management is definitely a heart issue. If we want God to trust us with the true riches of heaven and his true purposes for us on this earth, we must discover how to live an openhanded life. We must live a life of generosity rather than a life of selfishness and greed. As we do, he will be able to bless and use us beyond what we ever thought possible.

As Luke says in Luke 16:11, "If you are untrustworthy about worldly wealth, who will trust you with the true riches of heaven?" The converse is also true. If we are trustworthy with worldly wealth, we will be trusted with the true riches of heaven. Being trustworthy means understanding that God owns it all, that we are managers, and that as part of our management we are called to live an openhanded life of generosity. How do we get there? By scaling the generosity ladder—which begins with baby steps toward excellence.

Baby Steps

In his famous letter to the believers in Corinth, Paul wrote, "Since you excel in so many ways—in your faith, your gifted speakers, your knowledge, your enthusiasm, and your love for us—I want you to excel also in this gracious act of giving" (2 Cor. 8:7). Paul's words may be a little confusing to you. First of all, why did he say, "gracious act of giving"? Second, what does it really look like to excel in giving?

As we've established, giving is not always easy. If we

If we want God to trust us with the true riches of heaven and his true purposes for us on this earth, we must discover how to live an openhanded life.

aren't living under the right paradigm, we won't want to let go of what has been given to us. We have a natural instinct to keep our fist tightly closed over the peanuts. So giving in the way God wants us to give requires grace— grace he provides as we begin to trust his ultimate control over our financial life. We need God's grace to get to each new level of the generosity ladder. No one makes the climb in his own power.

Now let's think about this business of excelling in giving. How can you excel in giving? Paul means that you become excellent at being a giver. You recognize the freedom that giving brings into your life. You strive toward generous living through generous giving. You have a desire to give, and you do it cheerfully.

But maybe you're not there yet. Most of us have to learn to excel in this gracious act of giving by taking small steps toward excellence. If you think about it, everything you have ever excelled at came in stages. We can't go from zero to sixty without learning how to shift the gears in between.

This reality hit me one day—quite a while before the birthday surprise incident—as I was walking with my then two-and-a-half-year-old son through a park. He was stomping in mud puddles and doing all the things two-and-a-half-year-olds do when it dawned on me that he had mastered this thing called walking. That may not sound too impressive, but it hadn't been very long since he had entered what I like to call stage 1 of the learning to excel at walking process.

Stage 1 started when he was about six months old. One day, he taught himself how to move his body forward in an identifiable way. He would lie on his stomach and put his elbows out and scoot forward like an inch worm. I called it the army crawl. He couldn't stand up or walk yet, but he was getting started.

Then a little while later, he entered stage 2. Out of the blue he figured out how to make his arms and legs work together so he could crawl. And once he learned to crawl, he zoomed around so fast I couldn't keep up with him.

Obviously, as time passed, he had to advance past the crawling stage. He couldn't crawl around on his hands and knees forever. So he moved on to stage 3, which I like to call the wobbly baby phase. He learned to pull himself up and hold on to something to walk from one place to the next. He would lean on the couch and then somehow make his way over to the chair, using something solid to support himself as he went.

Then all of a sudden, one day he walked with confidence. He learned to excel at this new skill by going through a series of stages.

If you are going to learn to excel at anything in life— whether it's driving a car or learning a foreign language— you have to progress through a series of stages. The same holds true for learning to honor God with your finances.

The way we ultimately honor God with our finances is through our giving. As Paul put it, we learn to excel in the grace of giving. To excel is simply to become excellent at something. So how do you become excellent at giving in a God-honoring way? By going through giving stages, or as I prefer to think of it, by climbing the rungs of the generosity ladder.

Peace Pointers

As part of getting on the ladder toward peace with our finances, it's important that we:

- get out of debt
- create a budget
- break the bonds of materialism
- live within our means
- make wise financial decisions

For some helpful, free materials on each of the above points, visit www.GenerosityLadder.com.

3

mastering the basics

I ask you to begin giving, and to continue as you
began.... You'll find in the end that you got far more
than you ever had, and did more good than you ever
dreamed.

Stephen King

An inclination to give is written on your soul, no
matter how muted it may be by your present
concerns or lack of belief. Sometimes it takes a trau-
matic experience to bring that God-given pull toward
generosity to the surface. Horror novelist Stephen King
is not usually associated with sharing timeless biblical
principles. But in a commencement speech delivered

to Vassar graduates a few years ago, he offered some powerful insight on living an openhanded life. Here's an excerpt from his comments:

A couple of years ago I found out what "you can't take it with you" means. I found out while I was lying in a ditch at the side of a country road, covered with mud and blood and with the tibia of my right leg poking out the side of my jeans like a branch of a tree taken down in a thunderstorm. I had a MasterCard in my wallet, but when you're lying in a ditch with broken glass in your hair, no one accepts MasterCard.

We all know that life is ephemeral, but on that particular day and in the months that followed, I got a painful but extremely valuable look at life's simple backstage truths. We come in naked and broke. We may be dressed when we go out, but we're just as broke. Warren Buffet? Going to go out broke. Bill Gates? Going out broke. Tom Hanks? Going out broke. Steve King? Broke. Not a crying dime.

All the money you earn, all the stocks you buy, all the mutual funds you trade—all of that is mostly smoke and mirrors. It's still going to be a quarter-past getting late whether you tell the time on a Timex or a Rolex. No matter how large your bank account, no matter how many credit cards you have, sooner or later things will begin to go wrong with the only three things you have that you can really call your own: your body, your spirit, and your mind.

So I want you to consider making your life one long gift to others. And why not? All you have is on loan, anyway. All that lasts is what you pass on. . . .

We have the power to help, the power to change. And why should we refuse? Because we're going to take it with us? Please. Giving is a way of taking the focus off the money we make and putting it back where it belongs—on the lives we lead, the families we raise, the communities that nurture us.

A life of giving—not just money, but time and spirit—repays. It helps us remember that we may be going out broke, but right now we're doing O.K. Right now we have the power to do great good for others and for ourselves.

So I ask you to begin giving, and to continue as you began. I think you'll find in the end that you got far more than you ever had, and did more good than you ever dreamed.[1]

Who knows how familiar Mr. King is with the Old Testament. I wouldn't venture a guess. But intentionally or otherwise, his remarks on giving perfectly support the book of Ecclesiastes's observation: "We all come to the end of our lives as naked and empty-handed as on the day we were born. We can't take our riches with us" (5:15). They also echo the mind-set that takes the sting out of this condition, as spoken by Jesus in the New Testament: "It is more blessed to give than to receive" (Acts 20:35).

Basic-Level Giving

In the last chapter, we discovered that the way we honor God with our finances is through our giving, or by scaling the generosity ladder. But how does this generosity ladder actually work? How do we get on it in the first place?

As I mentioned, the generosity ladder is simply a tool to help you move from a life of financial stress to a life of financial peace (see fig. 3.1). The person on the ladder represents you. You get on the ladder by opening your hand—that is, by returning an initial gift to God through your local church. The decision to give gets you on the first rung—the rung of basic-level

Fig. 3.1 Rung #1: Return an Initial Gift to God

giving—which is the first step in the journey toward a life of blessing.

The key is to get started by giving a gift. There is nothing grand or complicated about it. Acting out of your new paradigm—acknowledging that your financial resources are actually God's and that you are just the manager—you decide to give a gift back to him. That gift gets you started; it gets you on the ladder. This is not a good place to stay, but it is a good place to start.

Giving for the first time can be scary. Even though you want to begin honoring God by bringing a gift back to him, you will inevitably have questions and doubts. What if you give and then you are strained financially? What if you can't make ends meet as it is? How will the money you give be spent? These are all questions that keep people from taking the steps toward a life of financial peace, and they are valid concerns with which many new givers struggle. We'll address some of these questions in the pages ahead.

This kind of struggle is part of the human condition. Day after day, we find ourselves in situations that put our head and our heart in conflict with each other. Even when we know what we should do, as in the case of giving, the fear of actually doing it sometimes paralyzes us.

The apostle Paul, who wrote much of the New Testament, understood our struggle well. He admits that he faced it in his own life. In Romans 7:21–25, Paul laments:

> I have discovered this principle of life—that when I want to do what is right, I inevitably do what is wrong. I love God's law with all my heart. But there is another power within me that is at war with my mind. This power makes me a slave to the sin that is still within me. Oh, what a miserable person I am!

As long as we walk this earth, we will be caught in a war that pits our faith in Jesus's ways against the "common-

---

Rung #1—Basic-Level Giving: Return an initial gift to God in a way that is identifiable and accountable.

---

sense" leanings of our nature. Many of this war's confrontations are played out on the battlefield of giving.

In *Fields of Gold,* Andy Stanley writes, "Fear has always been one of the principal enemies of a growing faith. It has a way of clouding our thinking and obscuring the facts. You may know precisely how God would like you to handle your finances, but fear has the potential to freeze you in your tracks or send you down another path."[2]

Fear keeps people locked in the lie of the scarcity mentality—the idea that the more you give away, the less you will have for your own needs. The only way to break out of the trap of that lie is to take the first step in faith: give an initial gift and get on the ladder.

As much as Paul understood the struggle we have with ourselves, he also knew that following God's commands and principles was not something to be left to feeling. Sometimes we just have to decide to get started with what's right, no matter how we may feel about it at the time. Emotions are fleeting, but God's truth about his plan for our financial lives is timeless.

Learning to Give

In 1 Corinthians 16:1–2, Paul writes, "Now about the collection for God's people. . . . On the first day of every week, each one of you should set aside a sum of money in keeping with his income" (NIV). In this short passage, Paul gives us insight into how we ought to bring our gift to God.

46

First of all, he talks about how much we are supposed to give: a sum in keeping with our income. The Bible never tells us to give a specific dollar amount. Never do we hear, "To honor God, you must give $100 every week." Of course not. The issue isn't a dollar amount but rather how proportional our gift is to our income.

Ultimately, giving is about our level of sacrifice. If you make just a little bit of money, you are expected to give only a little bit. If you don't make anything, you aren't expected to give anything. Your giving should be

Your giving should be directly and proportionally tied to what God allows to come into your life.

directly and proportionally tied to what God allows to come into your life.

College students have a lot of questions about this issue. Many want to give but don't have an income while they are in school. They'll approach me and say, "I want to give, but I don't know how much I should give since I don't have any real income." I always tell them that, biblically, they don't have to give yet. People with no income aren't expected to give. Still, I encourage them to give a little when they can, just to get on the ladder and begin establishing a habit for when they are blessed with an income, no matter how large or small.

Honoring God by bringing a gift back to him acknowledges his importance in your life. By choosing to return a gift to God, you are essentially saying, "God, I am thankful for the life, health, breath, and intelligence you have given me to be able to earn this money. Apart from you, I wouldn't have anything in my life. So I am going to honor you by returning a part of what you've given me."

Paul also tells us when we should give: on the first day of every week. This assertion gives us an opportunity to build a bridge of application between the ancient context of Paul's writing and our modern-day lives. In biblical times everybody was paid on the last day of the week, so they brought part of that income to the temple on the first day of the week. Pretty simple.

Things don't work out quite so well in our day. Some people are still paid at the end of the week, while others get paid every two weeks or once a month or once a year or when they close a big deal or when they land a gig. You get the picture.

So how can we apply Paul's instruction to bring our gift on the first day of every week? Look at the timeless principle in Paul's instruction: return a gift to God when you are paid. Not only that, but as the Corinthians did, we should return our gift in a way that is both identifiable and accountable.

Making Your Gift Count

When you decide to step out of financial stress and get on the ladder toward peace, make sure you give your initial gift in a way that is identifiable and by which you can be held accountable. That means, first of all, that when you give your gift to your local church, do it through whatever offering system the church has in place. If your church provides offering envelopes, make sure you give using an offering envelope. Or maybe you can give to your church online. Just make sure you give in a way that lets the church leaders know you gave.

People sometimes question this by bringing up Jesus's words in Matthew 6: "Watch out! Don't do your good deeds publicly, to be admired by others, for you will lose the reward from your Father in heaven. . . . Give your gifts in private, and your Father, who sees everything, will reward you" (vv. 1, 4).

Too many people think this passage means they should give without any kind of acknowledgment. But that's an incorrect interpretation. In reality, it means you shouldn't tell other people the amount you are giving. You shouldn't brag about the fact that you give or disclose the dollar amount of your gifts to your friends and relatives. In no way does it mean your church leaders shouldn't know.

Scripture goes on to tell us that those who have been appointed leaders within the church should know what people are giving back to God. In fact, Mark recounts the story of Jesus sitting by the collection box in the temple, watching as people brought their gifts (Mark 12:41). In the book of Acts, givers actually brought their gifts to the church and laid them at the pastor's feet (Acts 4:34–35 NIV). Aren't you glad we don't have to do that today?

Even though we have moved away from ancient methods of giving to more modern options like envelopes, online giving, and bank auto-debit, the principle remains the same. You must give your gift in a way that is identifiable to your church leaders. Why? So that they will be able to hold you accountable for your giving—not so they can lord it over you but so they can report back to you on what you've given and how it is being used.

There's another perhaps more important reason you should give in an identifiable and accountable way: doing so lets your church leaders know you have stepped on to the generosity ladder and puts them in a better position to help you in your climb.

Basic-level giving is a step in the right direction. It puts you on the ladder and begins prepping you for your climb. It is the jumping-off point. However, stalling at the basic-giving level would be like putting on your swimsuit, walking out to the pool, and spending all day with one toe in the water. You may have taken a step toward that crisp, fresh rush of water, but you have stopped short of the reward.

Once you have given an initial gift and stepped on to the ladder, it's time to move to the next stage of your journey toward excellence.

> I was once young and now I am old, but not once have I been witness to God's failure to supply my need when first I had given for the furtherance of His work. He has never failed in His promise, so I cannot fail in my service to Him.
>
> William Carey

4

being obedient

I never would have been able to tithe the first million
dollars I ever made if I had not tithed my first salary,
which was $1.50 per week.

John D. Rockefeller

Does the idea of the tithe make you uncomfortable? You aren't alone. Tithing is one of the most
misunderstood and argued about teachings in Christian
circles—but it's associated with biblical truth that can't
be ignored. Let's dig in and see what the Bible really has
to say about the tithe and how it relates to our climb up
the generosity ladder.

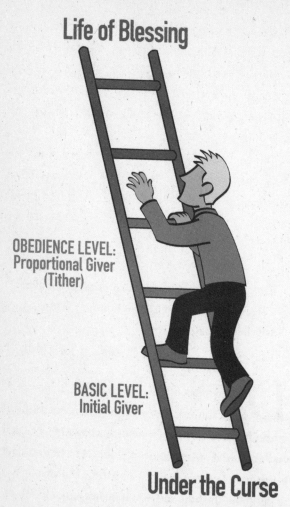

Fig. 4.1. Rung #2: Return the Full Tithe to God

The second rung of the ladder toward financial peace takes us to obedience-level giving. You step up to this level when you begin to return the full tithe to God on a consistent basis. As its name suggests, the obedience level is where you start being fully obedient to God with your finances.

Obedience-level giving is the core section of our ladder. It spans the majority of the gap between a life of financial stress, or "life under the curse" (which we will discuss momentarily), and a life of financial peace, or "life of blessing" (see fig. 4.1).

I am amazed by the number of people who have never studied the word *tithe*. They may have listened to what

---

*Rung #2—Obedience-Level Giv-
ing: return the full tithe to God.*

---

other people—including financially stressed relatives, co-workers, and friends—have said about the tithe, but they have never taken the time to go to the Bible to see for themselves what it says.

Even in the midst of this rampant ignorance, if you want to start an argument at the dinner table, bring up tithing. Few topics ignite the same kind of heated discussion. Why? Well, we've already established an inseparable link between a person's money and his heart (Matt. 6:21), so any dialogue dealing with the handling of personal finances strikes at the core of a person's being. As a result, the differing viewpoints on giving are charged with passion. Everyone's opinion is attached to his checkbook, so his heart is engaged. Let's see if we can find some clarity.

Obedience-Level Giving

Take a look at one of the most famous giving passages in all of Scripture: Malachi 3. In verses 8–10, God, addressing the people of Israel, says:

> "Will a man rob God? Yet you rob me. But you ask, 'How do we rob you?' In tithes and offerings. You are under a curse—the whole nation of you—because you are robbing me. Bring the whole tithe into the storehouse, that there may be food in my house. Test me in this," says the LORD Almighty, "and see if I will not throw open the floodgates of heaven and pour out so much blessing that you will not have room enough for it." (NIV)

In this passage, God clues us in to three important truths about the tithe. First of all, if we are not tithing, we are robbing him. Partial obedience is complete disobedience. That's why it is not a good idea to stay at basic-level giving. While it's a great place to get started, it's not yet in the realm of obedience.

Can you imagine if a husband approached his wife and asked, "Honey, have you been faithful to me?" and she replied, "Well, partially. I've only committed adultery half of the last fifty-two weeks." That wouldn't work, would it? Partial obedience is complete disobedience.

Let me take this opportunity to define the tithe, just to clear up any uncertainty. A tithe literally means the first tenth. We are commanded to return one-tenth of our income to God—but not just any tenth. We are to give back the first tenth of all God blesses us with each time we are paid. In Proverbs 3:9–10, Scripture teaches us, "Honor the LORD with your possessions, and *with the firstfruits of all your increase*; so your barns will be filled with plenty, and your vats will overflow with new wine" (NKJV, emphasis added). Giving leftovers won't do. God wants the best of what we have to offer.

Consider the Genesis 4 account of Cain and Abel. God comes to the two brothers and asks them to bring him an offering. Abel, who is a shepherd, immediately brings the best one of the firstborn lambs from his flock

---

We are to give back the first tenth of all God blesses us with each time we are paid.

---

and sacrifices it before God. But Cain, a farmer by trade, approaches God's command with a different attitude. Genesis 4:3 tells us, "When it was time for the harvest, Cain presented some of his crops as a gift to the LORD." While the Lord is pleased with Abel's gift, Cain's gift is not acceptable. In fact, the Lord says to him, "You will be accepted if you do what is right. But if you refuse to do what is right, then watch out" (Gen. 4:7).

What was the difference? Abel immediately brought God the firstfruits of his increase. Cain, when he was ready, brought God some of his increase. What we give God, and when, is a testament to the ordering of our heart's priorities.

The second thing we can learn from Malachi 3:8–10 is that those who are not tithing are not being fully blessed by God. Scripture actually tells us that non-tithers are "under a curse" (3:9). In other words, failing to tithe blocks God's ability to bless us to the extent he would like.

What does this curse look like in our culture? Here are a few of the trademark symptoms:

- Going to bed every night worried about money
- Arguing with your spouse over money
- Living in fear of losing everything

No man can mock God. We cannot ignore and dispute his plan for our livelihood and still expect to have his blessing on our life. But when we are obedient to the call to tithe, he will bless us in unimaginable ways—both financially and otherwise. I have learned firsthand that I would rather tithe 10 percent and live with God's supernatural blessing on the other 90 percent than to have the full 100 percent in my pocket and operate without God's blessing.

On a side note, one of the most frequently asked questions I hear about tithing is, "Should I tithe based on my gross income or my net income?" My answer is always the same: "Which amount do you want God to bless?" When you make a decision to tithe based on your net income, you are essentially putting the government in a position of priority over God. You are giving to him from what's left over after Uncle Sam takes his due. Giving based on what the government leaves behind is not a tithe.

Third, Malachi 3 is the only place in all of Scripture where God says "test me" in a positive way. He is essentially saying, "Bring me the tithe and see if I don't bless you. Go ahead. Try it." His challenge here is to Christians and non-Christians alike.

At the church I pastor in New York City, The Journey Church, we sometimes issue a tithe challenge to

---

We cannot ignore and dispute God's plan for our livelihood and still expect to have his blessing on our life.

---

people, and we direct it at both believers and nonbelievers. I teach what God says about the tithe, as we've been discussing here, and then ask people to test God in his promise by committing to tithe for a short period of time, usually four months.

In issuing the challenge, I will go so far as to say, "Hey, if you think you don't believe in God, isn't it worth a few dollars of your income over the next few months to prove once and for all that he doesn't exist? You are staking your eternity on this, so why not? Why don't you tithe for a few months, and if you still think God doesn't exist, you can live the rest of your life without having to worry about it." God said to test him.

Putting God to the Test

One time I met a gentleman at The Journey who was a self-professed agnostic. Let's call him Ben. Ben happened to be visiting with a friend one fall Sunday when I laid out this tithe challenge. Ben was a little older than our average attenders, and he was in the midst of a successful career as an air traffic controller.

After the service, Ben came over to me and said, "Okay. I'm going to test God. I want to take this 'tithe challenge' and dispel all this foolishness. I'm going to prove to you that God doesn't exist."

So he and I sat down and figured out what 10 percent of his income would be and divided that out over the next four months. He came to church a couple of times during the course of the challenge but not regularly. His tithing, however, was like clockwork. Can you guess what happened?

God worked in Ben's life in amazing ways. He began being blessed, both tangibly and intangibly. To make a long story short, Ben came back to me after those four months fully convinced of God's existence. Of course, as usually happens when someone takes the tithe challenge, he has continued to tithe.

Ben is not an exception to the rule. I have seen this scenario play out time and time again. God shows up in people's lives when they honor him. He has obligated himself to do so. God's promise about tithing is an if/then promise. "If you honor me with your firstfruits, then I will pour out my blessing in your life."

God's promise of blessing crosses over into the New Testament. Recall Jesus's "of course you should tithe" comment in Matthew 23:23. Paul follows that up in 2 Corinthians 8:7: "Since you excel in so many ways—in your faith, your gifted speakers, your knowledge, your enthusiasm, and your love for us—I want you to excel also in this gracious act of giving." As we excel in grace, we should excel in giving.

The Local Church

Often people question not the amount of a proper gift but where it should be given. Some people believe they should be able to distribute their tithe as they see fit. They want to control how their money is spent. If they aren't happy with the way their local church handles its finances, they think they should have the freedom to give their tithe to an outside organization. But Scripture teaches us that the tithe is to go to the local church—the one and only organization that is eternal. Offerings, any giving over and above the tithe, can be given outside the church, but not the tithe.

Let's look again at Malachi 3. God says to bring the whole tithe into the storehouse. Why? So "there may be food in my house" (v. 10 NIV). In biblical times, the storehouse referred to the temple. Today it is the modern church. The "food" God refers to is the ministry of the temple or, as we understand it, the ongoing work of God through his church on this earth.

In the New Testament church, givers actually laid their gifts at the apostles' feet, trusting them to distribute the money as God directed. Consider Paul's words in Acts 4:34–35: "Those who owned land or houses sold them, brought the money from the sales and put it at the apostles' feet, and it was distributed to anyone as he had need" (NIV). Can you imagine having to place your tithe at the feet of your local church leader? That would be intimidating, to say the least. Thank goodness we have more modern options for giving to the church—we can give at a service, online, or by mailing an envelope to the church office, to name a few—but the principle still holds true: we bring the tithe to our local, spiritually qualified leaders, and they distribute the money for God's work.

The tithe is specifically intended to infuse the local church so that God's kingdom can continue to expand at the best possible rate. It is not up to you and me as givers to judge where we'd like to give our tithe. We are simply told to make it the firstfruits, make it proportional, and bring it to the storehouse. In *Money, Possessions, and Eternity*, Randy Alcorn writes:

> I'm often asked, "But how can I give to my church [if] I don't agree with how the money is spent?" Perhaps your church leaders are in a better position to judge this than you are. . . . If the Bible tells me to pay taxes (Rom. 13:1–7), and I comply even though some will be wasted and even used for bad purposes, surely I can give to God even when I don't feel comfortable with every use of the funds.[1]

Of course, you do have to be wise. If you feel your church is operating in opposition to the Bible or truly misusing funds, you should talk to the leaders about your concerns. If you still don't feel comfortable tithing to your

---

The tithe is specifically intended to infuse the local church so that God's kingdom can continue to expand at the best possible rate.

---

church, you may need to begin seeking God's direction on finding a new church where you can give as he commands. A church leader's misuse of funds doesn't negate your call to tithe to the local church. Make sure you are in an environment where you can obey God fully.

The Blessing Zone

When you begin to be obedient by bringing the full tithe back to God, you move from being under the curse into the blessing zone. You put yourself in a position for God to be able to pour his blessing into your life, for him to begin replacing your financial stress with financial peace as you open your hand to him.

Tithing is about priority. When we bring the tithe back to God (note that we are bringing the tithe back to him rather than giving it to him; it was his to begin with), we are saying, "God, you are more important than my money. You have first place in my life." When you put God first in your finances, you will throw open the door to a life of blessing.

Once you get to this rung of the ladder, you will not want to climb back down. If you wear eyeglasses or contacts, you will be able to relate. Remember the first time you put on your new pair of glasses? Weren't you shocked by how clear and beautiful the world around

Tithing Worksheet

Ten percent sounds like an easy number to come up with, but many people never actually think through what their full tithe should be. Take a minute to complete this worksheet so you will know how to begin honoring God by returning the first 10 percent of your income to him.

- How much do I make in a year
  (before taxes)? $_____
- My yearly tithe should be (10%): $_____
- How much do I make in a month
  (before taxes)? $_____
- My monthly tithe should be (10%): $_____

you looked? Before, you probably didn't even realize you couldn't see. Once you experienced the world through the proper lenses, you never wanted to go back to muddled vision.

In all my years of helping people climb the generosity ladder, no one has ever said to me, "You know, tithing was a bad decision. I wish I'd never taken that step." Time and time again I have heard stories about how people are living more blessed lives on 90 percent of their income than they ever could have dreamed of on 100 percent. If you want to know God exists, start tithing. If you want God's blessing on your finances, start tithing.

The Tithing Debate

Some of you may be interested in diving a little deeper into the tithing debate. In broad terms, the divide over tithing comes down to a debate concerning legalism versus grace.

Opponents say that tithing, which has been in existence since the beginning of man (Gen. 14:20; Lev. 27:30–33) and was a command of the Jewish law (Num.

18:28–29; Deut. 12:11), was abolished when Jesus came on the scene. But Scripture confirms that Jesus came to earth to fulfill the law, not to dismiss it. Jesus himself minces no words when he says:

> Don't misunderstand why I have come. I did not come to abolish the law of Moses or the writings of the prophets. No, I came to accomplish their purpose. I tell you the truth, until heaven and earth disappear, not even the smallest detail of God's law will disappear until its purpose is achieved. So if you ignore the least commandment and teach others to do the same, you will be called the least in the Kingdom of Heaven. But anyone who obeys God's laws and teaches them will be called great in the Kingdom of Heaven. (Matt. 5:17–19)

Jesus shifted the heart of humankind from legalism to grace, but in doing so he in no way rendered the law obsolete.

I'm sure you are familiar with Jesus's most famous teaching, the Sermon on the Mount. Even if you've never read the account for yourself, I guarantee you know a lot about what he says. The words have become part of our culture. In this teaching, Jesus magnifies rather than minimizes the expectations previously associated with the law of Moses.

He says, and I paraphrase, "You've heard that you shouldn't murder. Well, I say don't even be angry with anyone. You know that you shouldn't commit adultery, but guess what? Under grace, you have already done so if you even look at a woman lustfully." The expectations Jesus places on his followers, thanks to the introduction of grace, go above and beyond the expectations of the law that preceded him.

If anger is now even with murder and lust is even with adultery, doesn't it stand to reason that the tithe should now be considered a base-level command—a minimum expectation now maximized through grace, like the other components of the law? Rather than being obsolete, giving under grace implies that we should give even more sacrificially than those who gave under the law; we should operate at a level higher than the threshold previously mandated.

Even under the bondage of the law, devout Jews often took it upon themselves to give God more than the first 10 percent of their increase. They recognized the truth that we've discovered in our paradigm shift: all they had came from God.

Logic would then suggest that we who have been given so much would also recognize the source of our blessings and feel even more inclined to return the tithe as an act of worship. After all, that's what tithing truly is; it's an act of worship. We should easily recognize 10 percent as simple obedience—like we recognize not murdering and not committing adultery as simple obedience—and be filled with the desire to give at least that much. Unfortunately, this is not the case.

The average modern-day Christian gives only 2.5 percent of his income, which obviously is nowhere close to a tithe. In *Money, Possessions, and Eternity*, Alcorn writes, "When we as New Testament believers, living in a far more affluent society than ancient Israel, give only a fraction of that given by the poorest Old Testament believers, we surely must reevaluate our concept of 'grace giving.' And when you consider that we have the indwelling of the Spirit of God and they didn't, the contrast becomes even more glaring."[2] We seem to have a heart problem.

Could the problem be that, deep down, many of those who oppose the tithe do so not out of biblical knowledge, prayer, and deduction but out of misinformation or out of their own sinful (perhaps even subconscious) desire to be the master of their money?

Their hearts are tied to their wallets, as are all of ours, and the contents of those wallets aren't being poured into God's work. So it makes sense that their hearts—far from understanding the supernatural blessings associated with the practical funding of God's kingdom—are waging a war for financial control.

As a result, they fight against the tithe. They call tithing outdated and legalistic. Even if only subconsciously, they feel that if they can discount the biblical mandate for twenty-first-century Jesus followers to tithe, then they can continue to handle their money as they please. The majority of these people are not intentionally choosing to be selfish. They are just caught up in a problem of the heart—one that is often caused more by a lack of knowledge about the tithe than by willful disobedience.

Alcorn goes on to say, "The Israelites' tithes [often] amounted to 23% of their income—in contrast to the average 2.5% giving of American Christians. This statistic suggests that the law was about ten times more effective than grace! Even using 10% as a measure, the Israelites were four times more responsive to the Law of Moses than the average American Christian is to the grace of Christ."[3] Let that sink in. Do you think that's what Jesus intended when he said he didn't come to abolish the law but to accomplish it? He calls us to go deeper and higher in our pursuit of God's desires, not to use his presence as an excuse to fall beneath the bar set by the law.

Tithing opponents rely most heavily on the argument that we are free from the law, that we have the liberty of giving to the God of our salvation through grace—and that is a true argument. One hundred percent undeniable. But a piece of the puzzle they are putting together is missing.

While they purport tithing as legalism, we are, by and large, living lives of stress and struggle. Our finances are out of control. We never seem to have enough, so we eagerly buy into their claim that we don't have to tithe. That means more for us, right? Wrong.

The missing puzzle piece begins to take shape with Jesus's words "of course you should tithe and you shouldn't leave the more important things undone either" (Matt. 23:23). He addresses tithing as something so understood that it's almost unworthy of mention. We are free from the law, yes. We have been called to live by the higher standard of grace.

Sometimes we just need to take a step back and examine why we believe what we do. What substantiates our positions? How do they measure up with God's reality?

Financial Peace

When you begin tithing, God's spiritual laws kick into high gear. Since you are honoring him, he honors you. I'm not promising his blessings are always going to be tangible. But they will be there, tangible and intangible.

Strangely, people who tithe have more money left at the end of the month than people who don't; people who tithe are able to pay off credit card debt and student loans faster; they have peace and security when difficult financial times hit; they are able to save for the future and for their children's education. God's Word is true. "Test me in this."

People often say to me, "I'm praying about whether I should tithe." Well, I don't want to discourage anyone from praying, so go ahead and pray. But as with so many other issues, Jesus has already given us the answer. In Matthew 23:23, Jesus says, "You should tithe." The answer is right in front of us, from the one who was our perfect example. Yes, you should tithe. If only all prayers were so easily answered!

In my office I have a file cabinet full of testimonies from people who have taken the tithe challenge and seen the reality of God's promise of blessing. Here are just a few of them:

> I have been distant from my parents and knew I needed to go home to visit. I make pretty good money, but because of my debt there was no way I could manage the trip. Although travel at my level of the company I work for never happens, my company sent me on a trip soon after I took the tithing challenge. Where did they send me? To the town where my parents live!—AR

> When you asked us to take the tithing challenge, my first thought was, "Yeah—right!" I work at a restaurant and just barely make ends meet. I knew it was the right thing to do, though, so I took the challenge. Soon after, I got the job that I had been pursuing for over six months.—AH

> I don't have any stories about how money for something I really needed suddenly appeared. I think the best thing that has come out of this is that God has given me the strength to really see that I already have so much and should take the time to appreciate what I do have.—CC

Since I took the tithing challenge, I have really stuck with it, and God truly has blessed me! Before, when I would tithe (or try to) I would always skimp short because I was afraid of not having money to make ends meet if I gave up that money. Since I have been tithing, I have really just put my faith in God, and he has completely come through, and then some! I definitely plan to complete the challenge and to continue tithing even when it's over. This has really opened my eyes to just have faith in God to take care of things that I can't control. I'm trying to do the same thing in other areas of my life too.—SN

God has been really testing my faith in ways that I never would have thought since committing to tithing. I have actually had trial after trial from finances, to my job, to my personal life. But God has grown my faith a great deal. And although it has hurt more than a little, my faith has grown more than I would have imagined.—LC

Within one week of making the commitment to honor God with my finances I was given an amazing career advancement opportunity with an annual raise of about 25 percent.—CJ

These people took the challenge, climbed to the obedience-level rung, and opened themselves up to a life of blessing. Are you ready to do the same? (For more on the tithe challenge, how you can take a four-month tithe challenge,

The 70-Percent Principle of Lasting Wealth

Imagine that a sum of money (like your paycheck!) comes into your life. What do you do? First of all, you don't close your fist around it; you keep your hand open and thank God for it. Then you tell it where to go:

If you are not in debt . . .

- The first 10 percent goes to your tithe.
- The second 10 percent goes into savings.
- The third 10 percent goes toward investments.

If you are in debt . . .

- The first 10 percent goes to your tithe.
- The second 10 percent goes to pay off debt.
- The third 10 percent goes into savings.

One of the major keys to reaching financial peace is this: learn to live on 70 percent of your income.

For more detailed teaching on this principle or for more information about wise financial planning, see www.GenerosityLadder.com.

or how you can implement it at your church, visit www.
GenerosityLadder.com.)

> What would happen if we accept God's gift of tithing
> when we accept God's gift of money? If we give off the
> top, we claim our place as "givers" before we admit that
> we are "consumers." That puts our priorities in order
> and establishes a framework of gratitude around the
> rest of our financial affairs.

> Henry Morris

5

living a life of extravagance

It is through generous giving, that we affirm before the world, our nation's faith in the inalienable right of every man, to a life of freedom, justice and security.

Harry S. Truman

What's your purpose on this earth? Do you know why you are here? Is it to build a career? A family? A nest egg? What wakes you up each morning and inspires you to face the day with expectation? For too many of us, the answer is simply "nothing." Or "obligation." The need to put food on the table. But that's not how God intended for us to live.

In his book *Run with the Horses*, Eugene Peterson remembers the time he saw a mother bird teaching her three young swallows how to fly by pushing them off a long, dead tree branch:

> [The] adult swallow got alongside the chicks and started shoving them out toward the end of the branch—pushing, pushing, pushing. The end one fell off. Somewhere between the branch and the water below, the wings started working and the fledgling was off on his own.
>
> Then the second one.
>
> The third one, however, was not to be bullied. At the last possible moment his grip on the branch loosened just enough so that he swung downward, then tightened again, bulldog tenacious.
>
> The parent pecked at the desperately clinging talons until it was more painful for the chick to hang on than risk the insecurities of flying. The grip was released and the wings began pumping. The mature swallow knew what the chick did not—that it would fly—that there was no danger in making it do what it was designed to do.
>
> Birds have feet and can walk. Birds have talons and can grasp a branch securely. They can walk; they can

cling. But flying is their characteristic action and not until they fly are they living at their best, gracefully and beautifully.

Giving is what we do best. It is the air into which we were born. It is the action that was designed into us before our birth.

Some people try desperately to hold on to themselves, to live for self. They look so bedraggled and pathetic doing it, hanging on to the dead branch of selfishness and self-centeredness, afraid to risk themselves on the untried wings of giving. Yet many people don't think they can live generously because they have never tried.[1]

You were born with an innate spirit of ever-increasing generosity, as much as those baby birds were born with an innate sense of flight. You were born to live a generous life. Maybe you've felt that truth pecking at your heart for years but have been afraid to let go of the branch. Or maybe this is a new realization for you.

When you and I discover how to live generously, we are free to soar into the life of blessing God wants us to live. But how do we let go of the branch? How do we flex our wings and fly? By first climbing up to our final perch on the ladder: peak-level giving. (See fig. 5.1.)

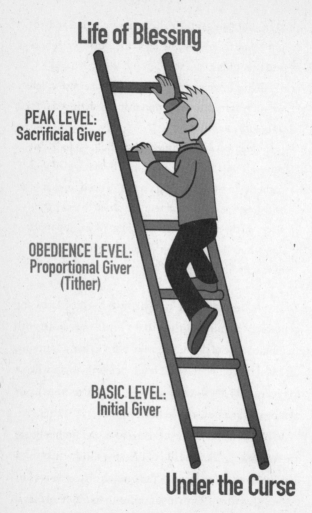

Fig. 5.1. Rung #3: Become a Generous Giver

Peak-Level Giving

You move up to peak-level giving by becoming a generous giver, by acknowledging the pull toward openhandedness within you and taking the step to live a generous life—not a life of disobedience or minimum requirements but a life running over with the spirit of generosity.

A generous life is characterized by three main things:

1. A willingness to stretch yourself. Instead of giving the minimum tithe every year, you stretch yourself to take even larger steps of faith. What kind of giver does

---

Rung #3—Peak-Level Giving:
become a generous giver.

God want you to be? Is he stretching you to give 11 or 12 percent each year? Maybe even 15 or 20 percent?

You should be willing and eager to set giving goals for yourself. Look at what you gave in the last year and say, "I gave X last year, so I am going to stretch myself to give X + Y this year." In 2 Corinthians 9:7, Paul says, "You must each decide in your heart how much to give.

And don't give reluctantly or in response to pressure. For God loves a person who gives cheerfully."

2. A desire to be generous with others. When you see need around you, you are quick to help. Rather than asking yourself, "Do I need to help that person?" you automatically give to his need. Being able to live in a place of quick generosity shows that you are controlling your money, not the other way around.

3. A decision to use your income fully to accomplish God's purposes in the world. Philemon 1:6 tells us, "You are generous because of your faith. And I am praying that you will really put your generosity to work, for in so doing you will come to an understanding of all the good things we can do for Christ."

The only way to understand fully how you can use your life and your finances to honor God is to step up to the rung of peak-level giving. Second Corinthians 9:6 makes this promise: "Remember this: Whoever sows sparingly will also reap sparingly, and whoever sows generously will also reap generously" (NIV).

Think about the people around you. Who in your life has modeled this kind of openhanded generosity for you? Who has excelled in the grace of sacrificial giving? If you can't think of anyone, then God may be calling you to set a new example among your friends and relatives. Will you be the one to step up to the top rung on faith and encourage others to make the climb?

I have been fortunate to become friends with some people who epitomize these three characteristics of generous living. I've seen what generosity has done in their lives, and it has motivated me to stretch myself.

One early mentor and friend of mine, in particular, has been an inspiration for generous living. You may have heard of the book *The Purpose Driven Life*. It was written by a pastor in Southern California who had no idea he was writing a book that would become the best-selling

---

The only way to understand fully how you can use your life and your finances to honor God is to step up to the rung of peak-level giving.

---

hardcover of all time, next to the Bible. He thought he was just writing a little book that would help some people reorient their lives toward the purposes of God. But God had other plans.

Within a few months of its release, *The Purpose Driven Life* sold over one million copies. To date, it has sold over forty million copies in English and over sixty million copies worldwide. Pretty unbelievable. Those sales naturally bring with them some monetary reward.

When my friend got his first royalty check, which was quite large, I asked him, "What are you going to do with all the money this book is generating?"

He answered, "I'm not sure yet, but I am searching Scripture to see what God would have me do."

Not too many weeks later, he called me and said, "I have decided to do four things. Number one, I've decided not to change my lifestyle. In other words, I'm not going to sell the house I've lived in for twenty years and buy a place in Malibu. I'm not going to sell my ten-year-old Ford and get a limousine. I'm going to keep my lifestyle the way it is."

"Second," he continued, "I am going to set up two foundations, one to help hurting pastors around the world and the other to help hurting children who have been orphaned by the HIV/AIDS pandemic. Third, I have decided to pay back to my church all the salary I've earned as their pastor for the last twenty years and continue pastoring for no income."

Needless to say, I was already so shocked by these first three decisions that I couldn't imagine what the fourth was going to be.

"Finally, I have decided to become a reverse tither." I honestly didn't know what he meant.

"The Bible says you are supposed to bring 10 percent of your income back to God and live on 90 percent," he explained. "I'm going to flip it. I am going to bring 90 percent of my income back to God and live on 10 percent."

Talk about someone whose story challenges us to be generous givers! You may not be able to be a reverse tither, but maybe you could whittle away at that 90 percent. What is God calling you to? Could you live on 80 percent and give 20 percent? Part of committing to a life of generosity means asking these questions and allowing ourselves to be stretched and used by God.

But there's more. As Paul Harvey would say, "And now, the rest of the story. . . ."

When my friend and his wife married over twenty years ago, they made a decision to excel in the grace of giving. They climbed the generosity ladder, determined to live their lives under the canopy of God's blessing. What did this look like? Tithing was a no-brainer for them—a minimum command—so as soon as they were married, they started stretching themselves by giving an extra percent every year.

The first year of their marriage, they gave 11 percent. The second year, they gave 12 percent. The third year, 13 percent, and so on. Now, these were not wealthy people. At the time, my friend was a struggling young pastor just out of school. The yearly increase was always a huge step of faith. But it's one he wanted to take, based on the truth and promises of God's Word.

Through the years my friend's generosity—his open-handed living—had shown God that he could be trusted with worldly wealth. He had demonstrated that his heart was not tied to his money. He had learned to truly excel at giving. And then God chose him to write the second best-selling book in the history of the world.

I've heard my friend say, "I'm not surprised God wanted the message of this book to get out there; I'm just surprised he chose me to write it." I'm not. God chose him because he had shown he could be trusted with the inevitable, impending success. He had proven himself to be a faithful, generous giver.

You are probably not going to write the next bestseller. Neither am I. Odds are you and I are not in danger of having millions and millions of dollars flood into our lives. But isn't that a great model, no matter what our level of income?

Ask, "God, how can I be a generous giver right now? How can I best honor you with my financial life? What are you calling me to?" Maybe you need to take the step

---

Unless you learn to be generous with the resources in your life right now—no matter how meager they may seem—you will not be generous with your resources later on.

---

of increasing your giving by a percentage point every year. Maybe you can decide to consistently help people in need. You have the freedom to make those kinds of decisions when you choose to live at the peak level of giving.

One of the easiest traps you can fall into is to tell yourself you will give more when you have more. That's just not true. Unless you learn to be generous with the resources in your life right now—no matter how meager they may seem—you will not be generous with your resources later on. It's quite a bit harder to give 10 percent,

11 percent, or 12 percent of $200,000 than it is to give the same amount of $20,000.

While most people like to think it will be easier to give when they have more money to work with, the truth is that our needs, desires, and lifestyles tend to grow with our incomes. Establishing the spiritual discipline of openhanded living early on keeps people from procrastinating with regard to giving until they make the ever-elusive "more money." For most of those who haven't learned to give out of a small income, more money is not enough to make them generous. If you don't start with the $20,000, your money will only make its way farther into your heart as it increases.

Remember the new paradigm: your money is not yours. You are just a manager. God doesn't give us increase so that we can be more comfortable or advance our lifestyle. He gives us more so that we can give more. We are the conduits.

Generous Giving = Generous Living

Giving generously does not have anything to do with the actual dollar amount you give; it has everything to do with what that dollar amount is in proportion to your income. When you give over and above the minimum requirement, quickly and cheerfully, you are a generous giver, no matter where the decimal point falls.

Mark tells us an interesting story in his Gospel. One day, Jesus decided to go to the temple to watch as people dropped their money into the offering box. Contrary to our common thinking, he wasn't too impressed with the rich people who put in the large gifts. Let's look at how the story unfolds:

> Jesus sat down near the collection box in the Temple and watched as the crowds dropped in their money. Many rich people put in large amounts. Then a poor widow came and dropped in two small coins. Jesus

Living the Generous Life

Don't store up treasures here on earth, where moths eat them and rust destroys them, and where thieves break in and steal. Store your treasures in heaven, where moths and rust cannot destroy, and thieves do not break in and steal. Wherever your treasure is, the desires of your heart will also be.

Matthew 6:19–21

The Top Four Ways to Invest Your Treasure:

1. Give a full 10 percent.
   - "A tenth of all you produce is the LORD's, and it is holy" (Lev. 27:30).
   - "Yes, you should tithe, and you shouldn't leave the more important things undone either" (Matt. 23:23).
2. Give extravagantly.
   - Read how Jesus receives and praises an extravagant gift in Matthew 26:6–13.
   - "I assure you, wherever the Good News is preached throughout the world, this woman's deed will be talked about in her memory" (Matt. 26:13).
3. Give sacrificially.
   - "He will give you all you need from day to day if you live for him and make the Kingdom of God your primary concern" (Matt. 6:33).
   - "They gave as much as they were able, and even beyond their ability. Entirely on their own, they urgently pleaded with us for the privilege of sharing in this service" (2 Cor. 8:3–4).

How much will I commit to give extravagantly/sacrificially over the next twelve months:

_____ percent above my regular tithes and offerings or

$ _____ above my regular tithes and offerings

4. Give cheerfully.
   - "I want you to be leaders also in the spirit of cheerful giving. . . . This is one way to prove that your love is real, that it goes beyond mere words" (2 Cor. 8:7–8).
   - "Each one should give what he has decided in his heart to give, not reluctantly or under pressure" (2 Cor. 9:7).

called his disciples to him and said, "I tell you the truth, this poor widow has given more than all the others who are making contributions. For they gave a tiny part of their surplus, but she, poor as she is, has given everything she had to live on." (Mark 12:41–44)

Whether you can best relate to the poor widow or to the likes of Bill Gates, you are called to be a generous giver right now, in your current circumstances. As you take that step up to the final rung, you will step into a life blessed beyond your wildest imagination. A world you never knew existed will be fully within your reach. Remember, you were created to give. Doing so is the air that allows you to soar.

> But those who trust in the LORD will find
> new strength.
> They will soar high on wings like eagles.
>
> Isaiah 40:31

6

taking your next step

> Make as much as you can, save as much as you can, and give as much as you can.
>
> John Wesley

One morning, a wise professor stepped into his classroom determined to prove a point to a bunch of sleepy students. Under his arm he carried a big, widemouthed jar. He made his way to the front of the room and placed the jar on his desk. With the students paying little attention, he filled the jar with five big stones. He put the stones in one by one until the jar couldn't hold anymore. Then he asked his students, "Is this jar full?" They half-nodded their assertion that it was.

The professor pulled a bucket of pebbles from under his desk. Slowly, he poured the pebbles into the jar. They bounced and settled into the small spaces that had been created between the stones. Once again, the professor asked his students, who were now slightly more awake, "Is this jar full?" They all quietly contended that, yes, of course it was.

The professor proceeded to pull another bucket from beneath his desk, this one filled with fine sand. As the students looked on, he poured the bucket of sand into the jar. The granules quickly filled in the barely visible cracks and crevices left between the stones and pebbles. This time when asked, "Is this jar full?" the class answered with a resounding, "Yes!"

In response to his students' certainty, the professor reached under his desk and brought out a pitcher of water. The students watched in amazement as the professor poured the entire pitcher of water into the jar.

Then the professor asked a different question. "What was the point of this illustration?"

A student in the back called out, "You were showing us that you can always fit more into your life if you really work at it."

"No, that's not it," the professor answered. "The point is that you have to put the big rocks in first, or you'll never get them in. These five rocks are your top priorities. Carefully consider what they are, get them set, and everything else will fall into place around them."

Starting the Climb

When setting out on any adventure, you have to know where you are, where you are going, and how to get there.

So the only question that remains is,
"Where are you on the ladder?"

Over the last few chapters, you've discovered what a life of blessing looks like and how to get there. So the only question that remains is, "Where are you on the ladder?"

Are you just getting started? Perhaps you have never given a gift before, and you are ready to give for the first time. Do you give sporadically, or even regularly, but not proportionally? Then you haven't quite made it to the obedience level. Maybe you are tithing already, but you

Financial PEACE

PEAK LEVEL:
Sacrificial Giver

OBEDIENCE LEVEL:
Proportional Giver
(Tither)

BASIC LEVEL:
Initial Giver

Financial STRESS

Fig. 6.1. Where Are You?

feel God calling you to greater generosity. You need to step up to the final rung. Perhaps you give sacrificially from time to time, but it's not a lifestyle. What is God calling you to?

Take a moment to think about your current level of stewardship. Then grab a pen and draw a picture of yourself on the ladder in figure 6.1. Place yourself on whatever rung is appropriate for you right now. Be honest; God already knows exactly where you are.

In helping people climb the generosity ladder, I have seen something incredible happen time and time again. As people move up the ladder, they move closer to God. Those who are at the obedience level and the peak level consistently tell me that their hearts grew closer to God every step of the way.

I have also seen that with every rung they scale, they find increasing significance in their life, increasing levels of happiness, increasing levels of intangible blessing. They have less debt, less bondage to materialism, and less stress. This makes sense when you think about it. After all, Jesus is the one who said, "It is more blessed to give than to receive" (Acts 20:35).

Not only that, but as we've learned by now, "Wherever your treasure is, there the desires of your heart will also be" (Matt. 6:21). As you give, you are becoming more like God. In turn, he draws you into the life of blessing and peace that only he can offer.

Love and Money

God is the ultimate example of a generous giver. He gave more than mere money; he gave his Son. The Gospel of John tells the story:

> For God loved the world so much that he gave his one and only Son, so that everyone who believes in him will not perish but have eternal life. God sent his Son into the world not to judge the world, but to save the world through him. There is no judgment against anyone who believes in him. But anyone who does not believe in him has already been judged for not believing in God's one and only Son. And the judgment is based on this fact: God's light came into the world, but people loved the darkness more than the light, for their actions were evil. All who do evil hate the light and refuse to go near it for fear their sins will be exposed. (3:16–20)

Giving is motivated by love. Because God loved us, he gave. Because we love him, we give.

As I mentioned earlier, no one is able to scale the generosity ladder in his own power. Every one of us needs the Spirit of God to work in and through us to break our innately selfish ways and help us step into the life of blessing. That power can't work in our lives unless we first give ourselves to God.

In 2 Corinthians 8:5, Paul writes, "They gave themselves first to the Lord" (NIV). The way you handle money is one of the most important aspects of your life. Your financial decisions will influence every other area

---

Giving is motivated by love. Because God loved us, he gave. Because we love him, we give.

---

of your life. The only way to truly honor God with your finances is to climb the ladder and become generous in giving, but to do that well you first have to climb off the throne of your own life.

We began this book by talking about a paradigm shift. Everything you have belongs to God; you are a manager. Let's take that truth even deeper. Everything you are belongs to God. He created you. So you wouldn't have to be separated from him either in this life or in eternity, he sent his Son to die for your sins. Through Jesus, he made a way for you to have a relationship with him. All you have to do is accept his offer of salvation.

If you have never given your heart to God, let me encourage you to pray this prayer with me:

Dear God, I believe you sent your Son to earth to give me a perfect example of love and to die for my sins. Thank you for giving to me so sacrificially. I acknowledge that I have lived my life apart from you. I have sinned against you. Please forgive me and come into my life. I want your peace and your presence. I give my heart to you. Show me what it means to love the way you first loved me. Thank you, God. In Jesus's name I pray. Amen.

If you prayed that prayer, congratulations! You are now a follower of Jesus. You just made the most important decision of your life. I know you have questions. I've put some resources for you—including a downloadable new believer's guide—on our website. Just go to www.GenerosityLadder.com. Welcome to the journey!

The Big Stones

Back to our professor. As he proved to his class, you have to put life's big stones in place first. Then the details will fill in around them. If you don't, the small stuff will consume you, and you'll never be able to fit the big rocks in. How does this apply to your climb up the generosity ladder? Let's break it down.

We've established that you honor God with your finances through giving—through excelling at each giving stage and learning to live an openhanded life. As you make your climb up the generosity ladder, five big stones need to be in place in your financial life. These stones will give you solidarity and grounding as you move through the stages—or up the rungs—toward a life of blessing.

Stone #1: Determine Your Priorities

Financial peace has nothing to do with how much you make; it has to do with how much you spend. When you put God first by honoring him with the tithe and by choosing to live within your means, you have your financial priorities in order.

Stone #2: Decide to Get Out of Debt

Getting out of debt is a process that begins with a decision. Decide that you are going to stop increasing your debt right now. Don't buy anything else you can't pay for, and put together a plan for paying down the debt you already have. (Visit www.GenerosityLadder. com for some debt-reduction tools.)

Learn to be content with what you have rather than obsessed with always getting more. As Hebrews 13:5 says, "Don't love money; be satisfied with what you have. For God has said, 'I will never fail you. I will never abandon you.'"

Stone #3: Discipline Yourself in Small
Financial Ways

Luke tells us that unless we are faithful in the small things, we won't be trusted to be faithful in large things (Luke 16:10). In light of this truth, you need to begin to discipline yourself in small ways. For example, commit to getting on and climbing the generosity ladder. Make the decision to get out of debt, as mentioned above, and stay out. Decide to cut back on something in your life and put that money toward gaining financial peace. For example, brew your own coffee instead of buying coffee every day. Take your lunch to work instead of going out for lunch. Use the money you save to pay down your debt, add to your savings, or give to a need. Small changes have a huge snowball effect over time.

Stone #4: Discover the Joy of Generosity

Generosity is a way of life. You don't have to wait until you reach the peak level of the generosity ladder to adopt the attitude of a generous giver. Practice living an openhanded life each and every day, not just with your finances but in all areas.

Stone #5: Adopt the Habit of Now

Take your next step today. There's always a reason to wait, but procrastination is dangerous. Napoleon Hill once said, "Procrastination is the bad habit of putting off until the day after tomorrow what should have been done the day before yesterday." The only way to break a habit is to do something now! I can guarantee that if you don't start giving today, a year from today you'll wish you had; if you do start today, a year from now you'll be glad you did.

An Eternal Perspective

Life is too short and too important to live with the constant stress, anxiety, and worry that come from not honoring God with your finances. Let me close with one more paradigm-shifting thought. Take a look at this:

The dot above represents your life, the number of years you are on this earth. The arrow represents eternity. Compared to eternity, our lives are like fleeting shadows, here today and gone tomorrow. The Bible actually compares our lives to the morning fog—here for a little while and then gone (James 4:14).

We will spend a lot more time in eternity than we will in this life. While the shortsighted person lives for the dot, the wise person has opened his eyes to the reality of the arrow. Consider again Jesus's words in Matthew 6:19–21:

> Don't store up treasures here on earth, where moths eat them and rust destroys them, and where thieves break in and steal. Store your treasures in heaven, where moths and rust cannot destroy, and thieves do

not break in and steal. Wherever your treasure is, there the desires of your heart will also be.

I encourage you to memorize these verses and decide to live by them.

At the end of your life, your relationship with money will be summed up by one of two words, either *generosity* or *greed*. You have the opportunity, and now the tool, to embrace a life of generosity—a life free from stress and anxiety, a life in which your needs are met, and, ultimately, a life that honors God.

The decision is yours. The ladder is right in front of you. Are you ready to climb?

I am praying that you will put into action the generosity that comes from your faith as you understand and experience all the good things we have in Christ.

Philemon 1:6

notes

Chapter 2: Stepping toward Excellence

1. Randy Alcorn, *Money, Possessions, and Eternity* (Wheaton: Tyndale, 2003), 8.

2. Ibid.

Chapter 3: Mastering the Basics

1. Stephen King, www.stephenking.com/news_archive/archive_2001.html.

2. Andy Stanley, *Fields of Gold* (Wheaton: Tyndale, 2004), 15–16.

Chapter 4: Being Obedient

1. Alcorn, *Money, Possessions, and Eternity*, 246.

2. Ibid., 182.

3. Ibid.

Chapter 5: Living a Life of Extravagance

1. Eugene H. Peterson, *Run with the Horses* (Downers Grove, IL: InterVarsity, 1983), 23.

Nelson Searcy is the founding lead pastor of The Journey Church of the City with locations in New York City, Queens, Brooklyn, and Boca Raton, FL. He is also the founder of www.ChurchLeaderInsights.com. He and his church appear routinely on lists such as the 50 Most Influential Churches and the 25 Most Innovative Leaders. Searcy lives in New York City.

Jennifer Dykes Henson is a freelance writer based in New York City. She has served as a writer/producer and ministry consultant to organizations across the East Coast. Prior to moving to New York, Jennifer worked with Dr. Charles Stanley as the manager of marketing communications for In Touch Ministries in Atlanta, Georgia.